Singing The Middle Ages

Singing The Middle Ages

Poems

Tom Smith

The Countryman Press
Woodstock, Vermont

The following nineteen poems have appeared in: BELOIT POETRY JOURNAL (Winter 1959-60), Francesca da Rimini; AUDIENCE (Autumn 1960), Singers & Recipe; THE AMERICAN SCHOLAR (Spring 1961), Rosetree at Dawn; EPOCH (Winter 1961), The Moon & Carol; THE MINNESOTA REVIEW (Winter 1962), A Game of Snow; CHICAGO REVIEW (Winter-Spring 1963 & Autumn 1963), Lady Asleep, Brown-eyed Susan, & May; THE FAR POINT (Spring-Summer 1970), Catfish; BEYOND BAROQUE 771 (March 1977), Love Death, After Villon: The Dead Ladies, & Seven Salvations: A Mixed Bag; THE SMITH 20 (Summer 1978), Limerick Hagiograph; CAROLINA QUARTERLY (Winter 1978), Fox and Bee; BEYOND BAROQUE (10th Anniversary Issue, December 1978), Sisters; VIRGINIA QUARTERLY REVIEW (Autumn 1980), Why Birds Sing; DARK HORSE (Fall/Winter 1980), Burning Leaves: The Spinster.

Library of Congress Cataloging in Publication Data

Smith, Tom, 1933-
  Singing the middle ages.

  1. Middle Ages — Poetry. I. Title.
PS3569.M5384S5   811'.54   82-2452
ISBN 0-914378-87-2   AACR2
ISBN 0-914378-88-0 (pbk.)

Copyright © 1982 by Tom Smith

Manufactured in the United States of America

for my wife
VIRGINIA

Blyssid be the tyme
That appil take was!
Ther-fore we mown syngyn,
"deo gracias!"

Note

The poems in this volume have been written variously over a period (1953-1979) of twenty-six years and, though I have been aware in most instances of taking inspiration from the middle ages, it has only recently occurred to me how continuously I have been thus inspired; that these separate poems belong together. They build on themes, images, meters, and forms of the medieval period generally, sometimes of specific works. For instance, the opening and penultimate stanzas of "A Game of Snow" imitate the stanza of THE SECOND SHEPHERDS PLAY; and the images of star and tennis ball and cherry bough and bird, together with the shepherd MAC, have been transported out of that remarkable folk celebration of the nativity into my own twentieth-century world where they have magically merged with some quite real undergraduates observed from a quite actual seminar room during a quite perfect snowfall, in New Jersey, in 1958.

When I bring these pieces together they seem to me not only to sing but in some measure to evoke a world in which lyricism and whimsy strangely combine, prettily, playfully, but always ready to open a perspective upon hell or heaven.

I recognize it now: it is the middle ages, my middle ages, my self.

Contents

Singing The Middle Ages

Flower Studies

A Flower Calendar: (1) Tigerlily

The shower on the slender air
burdened the air like a flower.
Showers are flowers. The slender air
bloomed too. Ah! flowers, flowers —

We played a wheel at Primrose Fair,
I won a porcelain jar.
I put you in. I kept you there
and kept you as you were.

Gray maples scuffed the college square.
Their budding wore the hour.
Remember when the college square,
at Eastertime, was ours?

The lawns were bright with crocus spears,
with pretty crocus flowers.
April, laughing back salt tears,
at Eastertime was ours.

We didn't go home at Easter. We did
not go home at all, Lily.
I bought a bag of apples. We stayed
in College Hall, Lily.

We had our share of apples then,
Lily, the largest size.
The sun was in the sky again.
Lily, we saw it rise.

Tulips bled across the lawn
their crowns and crimson linings.
Tiger, I see you have put on
a king's crown shining.

Lily, you sing. I'm singing too:
"a bird is nailed to a tree."
Lily, you sing. It's all you do,
and all you will do for me.

A Flower Calendar: (2) Brown-eyed Susan

The elm grows tall, a dainty, lusty fellow.
A beggar's the willow.
The poplar bows, his eminence, a stranger.
I know I'm in danger.
I dare not leave my unguarded body sleeping
near lecherous trees. The branches harden dripping.
Ripeness is all a rape.
My body asleep,
I dream my pretty eyes are washed with weeping.
I eat the air, exhale
catches of swallowtail.

A Flower Calendar: (3) Bittersweet

I'm frightened, Tiger, by the crown
of burning leaves you have put on.

The rain will wash my crown away.
I fear the rain won't fall today.

I've apples, soaked, to quench your thirst.
Oh, Tiger, we will be ashes first.

My burning never burned so fast.
The largest apples fade at last.

See! What a crown my Lily wears!
Who's dropping apples by my ears?

I've dropped beside you on my knees.
I knew I shouldn't sleep near trees.

A Flower Calendar: (4) Holly

My lover held a nest of robins in his mouth.
The nest became a posy at my breast.
His robins bloomed. His blossoms ventured south.
We were a nest
of robins singing nightly to our rest.

My lover chooses now to go
and step like ashes to the snow's
apostasy.
O! Christmastree —

The 101 Dreams of Briar Rose

She dreams the world
is turning toward
her slumber: (1) her nurse,
tucking in linen, smoothing
embroidered silk, stops
quaintly bent, a thorn
tree nodding over her.
(2) Her little dog
across her feet and ankles
like a rug and (3) the fire
on the grate, then (4) the curtains
on the breeze and (5) the breeze:
all sleep.

At a casement (6) a moth,
(7) some fleas like motes
and (8) a beetle
like her father's signet
hang fixed upon the glass,
the air, her finger.

(9) The chitter and rustle of rats
and mice inside the walls fall silent.

(10) Bats, newly abroad
in quest of insects, swim
through twittering spirals back
to the dim suspence of eaves.

(11) Owl and nighthawk hover.
(12) Fieldmouse and rabbit cower.
(13) The raccoon lifts a fish
stilleto in his little fist.

(14) At the still point
where water meets earth and air
the otter poses a question,
sinuous, suggestive.

(15) Her father's park,
poplar and elm and willow,
grass and white gravel,
fox and antlered stag, swan lake,
spirals — O gradual
between her body and the moon.
(16) The moon stands still.
The roses quiver, leaves,
pricking like cat's ears,
alert and

(17) the last of her parents'
guests arrive. The sparkle off
their emerald carriage slows
to sheen. (18) The horses'
legs soften and merge
with darkness, hooves suck
the earth like snails. (19)
A footman bows, gloved hand
on the golden handle; (20) the door
half-opened, a braceleted arm remains
extended toward a waiting servant.

(21) The chessboard
of the stair beneath the stars
expects the players.
(22) The stars
look on, eternal
behind her lidded flesh.
Still (23) owls grasp the yawning air
staring. The roses gather.

(24) The great hall and the ballroom glitter,
then glare as (25) the candles flicker,
flare and freeze. There! — (26) Two butlers
have collided in a narrow door.
(27) A glass half topples from a tray.
The wine wells over, red
drops point and nearly reach the floor.

(28) Strings and a harpsichord pluck
and draw one note: a drone, an echo. (29)
The waltzers orbit. Muscular
thighs (30) attenuate in gorgeous
stockings. (31) Swift skirts ring Saturn, wing
and light the seraphim.
(32) Beyond the dance, centripetal, the lords
and ladies hang on studied gestures
like espaliered grapes while (33)
a child plays hide-and-seek among the gowns
and tablecovers, (34) another, (35) another
still.

(36) The roses swell.
The King, her father, keeps his throne.
Above the crowd, her father and his throne
together seem about to spring — a sphinx
crouching. Then (37) boys, attendant, crumple,
drooping heads across his knees. Look! —

(38) Downstairs, the ladle
drops into the soup, surges
and topples, floats
clockwise among the carrot moons
and (39) the steam stands like a veil around the cook.
(40) Sweat pebbles her brow and cheekbones.
(41) The fire baits and (42) the cat
sits at her feet like a coal
except that (43) his tail
switches over cobbles. (44)
So many: men and women, child and crone,
etch the curious postures of their service,
their shadows like an acid, on the walls
and furniture in kitchen, pantries, narrow halls
and broad, the wildering
of (45) flat silhouettes climbing the stairs.

Now — (46) The Queen,
threading her startled ear with golden wire,
catches her reflection in the looming glass.
She's caught. The roses grow.
(47) The roses overtake the fox.

The world's mosaic as her dream.
(48) In her ears the music hangs like a pattern of stars.
(49) Her feet and ankles swarm and sing their numbness.
(50) Her knees cool to her gown.
(51) The beetle's lifted wings upon her finger wait.
(52) Her hips dimple, (53) her breasts
ride, (54) she is
a craft of silk and linen limning:
(55) elbow and clavicle and wrist are scalpel.

(56) Her hair and nails explore her world, the dream.
(57) The otter poses in a crown of leaves and thorns.
(58) The cat's tail switches (59) and roses
burst from the horse's forefoot on the smith's
dark hand (60) and hold the pail of oats against
the stable boy tugging, the whippet's nose
nudging his buttocks. (61) She winces. Not even
the prince, her brother, could uproot
or rein her now. She's got it all. She stores
it wholly, her body's horde and fairy
walnut of her brain.
The thieves arrive.

(62) A child
peeps from the branches. (63) The looming mirror
shivers and, with it, the Queen. (64) The sphinx
glances askance and tautens. (65) The cat's
tail swipes rough stone.

        Then (66) a youth
appears — leaving the loose knot of his friends
in green and brown who (67) fade into the wood
with bow and arrow, falconed wrist.

(68) A youth approaches looking back —
the wood all green and brown and (69) a tall
youth wades through hawkweed and cinquefoil.
(70) A blond youth steals along the wall.
(71) A golden stallion, wonderfully garbed,
stops at the rose gate. (72) A silver
youth dismounts.

(73) The roses stiffen. (74) The cat unsheathes
poignant, opinionating talons. (75) A youth
tugging the rosestem, (76) a foot
testing a bough, (77) gloved
hand crushing a blossom, (78) another,
(79) another still and (80) still
another.

(81) Everywhere — hands
and feet and
(82) the swarming.

(83) The wood beyond her father's
garden heaves and (84) the forest
whirls around the park, the palace.
(85) Her heart pounds toward her brain
(86) a crimson saturation: (87) his red
hair and stockings, (88) his blood
and (89) the roses.
(90) Arms and legs.

(91) A youth stands, silent, amazed
among the lords and ladies. (92) A youth
turns slowly threading their dreaming figures
to the center of the room. (93) He stares
upward at the King. (94) He climbs
and (95) he passes
her mother's bedroom
quickly,

(96) he stops above her, bowing (97)
like a sapling in the draft
commencing from the window,
bending him toward her brow.

(98) Her hand interposes. (99) The beetle
struggles on its back. (100) Her little
dog stretches and sets to yapping.
She hears male laughter. (101) She dreams
that she is going to the ball.

Burning Leaves: (1) The Spinster

I wooed the Church with apples.
Seven priests had nervous breakdowns
striving with the beasts I loosed upon them.
Thirty years I sought out theologians.
Thirty years I fought them.
Then my mind agreed to go,
a bride, into the Church
where seven priests had died
for me. I knew no other men.
Meanwhile I taught
meeting the classroom with a smile: meekly —
but they have seen me grow to thought and fiercely
pin beneath my huntress foot
the body: Abelard, Villon
whose blood I brought to life
ripe as their own.
Now I retire. The leaves
exalt my name with fire.

Burning Leaves: (2) The Groom

Now we are married.
Woman, we are wed.
The sheets have twice been changed
on our bed.
Since leaves have fallen
brilliant in the street and dirty,
I shall have to wash my feet.
I've walked upon dead leaves.
I had no fear.
The rumor of our marriage
filled the air.

Rosetree at Dawn

Unformed to show an antique vase,
white roses on a table have
a look of wash or haze.

The rosetree's stricter branches carve
stiff niches where its virgin blooms
adorn this morning's nave.

Only one bee invades their bosoms,
taut pearls of scent and holiness,
and sings the white of blossoms,
sings of boughs and, only less
exact than stone, the rosetree is
a morning star of wood and rose
and rose to which the tree aspires,
its saint.

       Petals caress
each cloistered recess of pearl-white fires,
growing, until each bud is swarmed
and spread by ruining choirs
of bees, obscured as it is warmed
and sunshine bursts the star by too
much light, or too much love, unformed.

Bestiary

Fox and Bee

Foxes in cherry trees,
bees in our hands.
Come to the wedding.

Foxes in cherry trees.
Bees in our hands
swarm at our bidding.

Foxes in cherry trees.
Bees in our hands
swarm to the budding.

Spread white linen in the sun.
Beat the pillows one by one.
Sweeten the bedding.

Fox from a cherry tree
sleeps in our hands.
Come to the wedding.

Singers

See a golden bird
upon a golden bough.
Our eyes are gilded now.

Cat

The cat sits inside looking out
or outside looking in
as serious as if a world
were going to begin.

The cat sits inside looking out
and hears a fly. She sees it.
She will paw it, tease it,
craw it, look about
as serious as if a world
had been put out.

The cat sits outside looking in
and hears my step. She sees me.
Should she claw, appease me,
maw me? Eyes and chin,
she's serious as if a world
had been done in.

The cat sits inside looking out
or outside looking in —
dead serious: a world
is going — going
to begin.

Catfish

When I see the cat's black lips pulled back at sleep,
his flake and feather fur like a baked fish on a platter,
I remember Mendel (1822-84) and Lombroso (1836-09) and my
    friend,
        Hesperidian
        and grinning, then
the candlelight and music and the meal.

Cannibal Mantis

Sainted Jade, while kin
perfect your skin,
petition me a hero
dressed for love and war,
a draft of flesh,
for I am poor.

Prick Song at Compline

The campus dogs, the campus dogs
run together,
stand alone
waiting outside the reflective
pane or wooden door,
dodge the unexpected
predictable crowd between classes,
follow Professor Plum
who follows his glasses
to the library, play tag
with a youth who offers his cap
and, at last, a kick.
Dismissed. The campus dogs
snooze and sometimes twitch
in the winter sunlight. Stone
steps beneath them seem almost
eternal, almost dumb
as the campus dogs. The campus dogs
run together,
stand alone
untouched by Math or Diction,
immune to History or Modern Fiction,
quite thoroughly undergraduate and very
contemporary.

The campus dogs, the campus dogs
mount each other
male on male.
Infrequently a bitch presents
an easy target for the unself-conscious,
probably unlustful dart. "Right on."
They don't intend a show,
have no intentions, only act
as dogs have always done,
sniffing a stranger's golden penny,

offering the sugary strawberry
to the possibly gartered leg
of Dr Rhubarb, Dean of Men,
running the Spring-pink tights of Susan
Reingold, our English-major poetess,
who keeps a face almost
unknowing, almost straight
as the campus dogs. The campus dogs
mount each other
male on male,
uninhibited by Grammar, Sociology,
and unaware of Deviant Psychology,
quite thoroughly undergraduate and very
contemporary.

The campus dogs, the campus dogs
scuff the grass
and leave the load
behind on path, on playing
field, on the Humanities Quadrangle,
on The Green, idyllic under oaks,
that slopes from Administration Hall
so eloquently to The Gates,
leaf-catching lawn that so unreasonably
pierces the secretary at an upstairs
window with hopes, regrets almost
poignant, potent almost
as the campus dogs. The campus dogs
scuff the grass
and leave the load,
not ethical, not metaphysical,
not curious, not even quizzical,
quite thoroughly undergraduate and very
contemporary.

Why Birds Sing

From what I know of their absurd
metabolism I fancy
some trill or chirp,
rumble or eructation
is inevitable.

Anyone out on a limb
or walking a wire
is liable to peep
or squawk. Anxiety
will whistle from whatever
hole's at hand.

Suppose I see something rather
like me up an opposing tree.
The throat tightens. Hope
and fear break through
reflexively.

It seems appropriate
laying an egg to cluck
the shape of things to come —
or coo to mime the oval
nudging one's breast.

From dreams of flight
I've come to darkness
shouting and after a plunge
gone warbling to the bottom of the pool.

If memory were not my mother,
could I keep silent in a bush
while night fell uncreating everything?

Would I stand mute
inside the rising of the day?

Phoenix

Heart bursts again but brings
the burden wrapped in wings,
the wings that will not break
from wood and grove.

She bursts from day to day,
from sky to sky and shy
of heaven lives. It's closer
than to die.

Recipe

Set silver cushions
under thorn,
a virgin to catch
a unicorn.

Lovedeath

A Game of Snow

Lord, but this weather is cold. The room
is hot and smells like a dirty broom:
Dust makes the heat a perfect womb.
O Christ, these others, I assume,
        like lectures more
or less as much as I.
Lord, how my nose feels dry,
cracking. Is snowfall why
        we're here?

The window of the seminar
reveals the snowfall like a star
that gathers earth and air together.
The window opens on the weather,
the new snow falling, with the old
mingling, beneath the trees in the field.
Freshmen, bright and red in woolen
sweaters, rough the drifts they've stolen
from each other; tumbling, they
rough each other through each play,
their football game, in heaped formation,
without a ball. Revelation
is a game of snow. "Hey, Mac!" The boys
gaze outward from the heaps to praise
the virgins from across the way
in winter's sweaters, passing by.

I'd praise them, though I do not go
to join them, giving them a bough
of cherries, white to match the snow,
a tennis ball, a red one though,
        to match their sweaters,
and a bird that sings
all winter — with white wings.
It is not thought, but things,
        that matters:

blossoms, tennis balls, and birds
that do not fade when touched by words.
They are not angels, after all,
these boys who race the gaining fall
of snow that's faster now: their shouting
across the sky — no more than shouting?

May

I'll let you see my funny knees, Lady.
      Huge trees, Lady,
have no such knots as these of mine. Lady,
      perhaps they'll shine.
They are enormous knees, you'll see, for I
will roll my trouser leg that high, Lady.
      The sun, Lady,
      will turn them brown
and, Lady, we'll run beneath the yellow sky.

The Moon

I gave my love in place of pearl
a pearl-bush heaped
with white racemes
of flowers to be kept
beside her as she slept
while nightly the moon grew slimmer
the virgin girl.

I gave my love in place of pearl
a pearl moth pale
on a silver pin
in wooden frame so small
to hang on her bedroom wall
while nightly the moon grew slimmer
the virgin girl.

I gave my love in place of pearl
three Indian snails
whose spiral shells
were lined
with pearl in brittle cells.
Nightly the moon grew slimmer
the virgin girl.

I gave my love in place of pearl
a pearl-hen speckled white
with tiny feet.
I gave my love a pearl ring bound
with gold to make her sleep more sound
and nightly the moon grew slimmer
the virgin girl.

And in return each spendthrift girl
the silly rose
gave me that blows
beneath the evergreen
on thorny boughs.
We made the moon grow great again as pearl.

Lady Asleep

Beside my waking moonlight keeps
her flesh and image clear. The curtain sweeps
where lady sleeps
across her yellow hair.
This rests my waking, watching where
she sleeps.

The moon that was a virgin shares
accomplishment with her. The moonlight wears
their common spheres
while lady lies asleep.
This peace I watch, but may not keep,
endears.

Her body in the moonlight reaps
the silence from the air. My hand that slips
as lady sleeps
this gauze away from her
can reach one moment's stillness where
she sleeps.

Francesca da Rimini

"Nevertheless,
although her dress was white and gold,
the girl has sinned; for she has held
huge ugliness

upon the slight
hold of her bright thighs, accepted
the grey husband into her bed,
permitting night

by leveling
its cordial blind to ease her task
(a darkness on what he might ask
of reveling)

before her sleep.
This is my case: this woman's was
the rose's face and beauty owes
its beauty keep.

Worldliness bent
Francesca down." Rose pressed to rose
and thorn crushed into thorn: love is
her punishment.

Serenade

Lady! Our garbage scow
slouches across the harbor heading
for high sea and a towering sunset.

Love Death

Below them central park
glitters bright and dark.
The sea bursts into time and never done
considers from the table
diminished betty grable
on portable tv.
Then, taut upon your breath and craft
your dress,
the napkin on his knee,
his scented hand — guerlain —
turning napoleon
and snifter from steuben
to mazda with a yawn:
the sea takes all our stone.
The waves that take Isolde to the sea
Isolde takes.

Below them central park
glitters bright and dark.
The sea bursts into time and never done
returns while maytag spews
forgotten. She draws
the blinds, her arms — chiffon —
and hem, hovering: *Then,*
coiled beneath banners and emblems, clay,
the shore, rock, death's head — all
your dying — all that love can say.
She shimmers there, behind
her, bland, the slatted blinds,
and — frosted rubinstein —
entices jockey, brooks, and hathaway:
am I the sea and mine
the craft of all our foundering
and all that love can say?

Below them central park
glitters bright and dark
and screams at coming headlights,
"Oh, those nellie hoods
are killing my sister—dead
she lies—dead in her beads."
The sea bursts into time and never done
takes all our stone.

After Villon: The Dead Ladies

Where? Tell me, Groovy, in what void
or vale of dollies — tabloid, gloss —
rolls Jayne perpetually employed
in capitable gain or loss?
Where's Judy? Garlanded across
what bluebird rainbow's reachless span
moans Lady Day remote as moss,
"Ah, Groovy, where's the old snow, man?"

Does platinum, does celluloid
strip Harlowe? Say — Do crow and cross
hawk Bessie Smith off trapezoid?
Does Eagles slip on golden sauce
along the luminary jaws
while Sylvia brings bees to Pan
and Marilyn like dental floss
coos, "Groovy, where's the old snow, man?"

Where's Mrs Woolf lighthousled, buoyed
on nightmare waves? What Trojan hoss
throws Isadora who enjoyed
Greek passes gossamer? Say, Boss,
where? Tell me — Where in tilt and toss
of pearl exploits whoops Joplin, Jan?
Where's Shirley Jackson? Haunting straws.
And, Groovy, where's the old snow, man?

Prince, ask again the snatch that gnaws
behind the wind. Prig, ask again.
The scything stars through dust and dross
sigh, "Groovy, where's the old snow, man?"

Sisters

Queen Guenever
Saint Joan
snatched from the fire
by Lancelot
by Jesus
wing Phoenix
into time & mind.

Two for Mother Goose

Where is She Now?

These are the pumps that Jane wore.

These are the feet —
how tardy! how fleet!
that walked in the pumps that Jane wore.

These are the knees
as dimpled as seas
that bent over the feet
that minced down the street
and stalked in the pumps that Jane wore.

This is the seat —
ah! wind in the wheat —
that swayed over the knees
as dimpled as peas
that bent over the feet
trochaic, that beat,
the heart in the pumps that Jane wore.

This is the frock,
a silk hollyhock,
caressing the seat —
all twitter and tweet —
that swayed over the knees
as round as her fees,
that bent over the feet,
still pointed as sleet,
that tripped in the pumps that Jane wore.

This is the waist
like scissors and paste
that bowed in the frock
of dickery-dock
embracing the seat
as pretty as Pete
that tucked under the knees
that jangled my keys
in the dash, and the feet
in the night and the heat
and the stars in the pumps that Jane wore.

These are the breasts,
the twin Everests,
that rose from the waist
and, so cleverly laced,
embarrassed the frock
with their tickery-tock
to the swing of the seat
rather low and the beat
pulsing back of her knees
that tingled and teased
and bent over the feet
of my darling, my cheat,
my despair. O the pumps that Jane wore.

This is the hair
flowing loose on the air
that plays round the breasts
like waves at their crests
swelling clean from the waist
that seraphs embraced.

Now torn is the frock
like a leaf from the stock
and this is the seat,
once saucy, once neat,
and these are the knees
like crackers and cheese
that crumbled, the feet
that struggled, the feet
that slept in the pumps that Jane wore.

These are the eyes
as busy as flies
when she tossed back her hair.
O how empty they are!
Unsupported the breasts
like two orioles' nests
hang almost to the waist
where cherubim traced
through the wash of her frock
strange enchantment, faint shock.
Yes, this is the sweet
and voluptuous seat
like the heaven of bees
and these are the knees
that pleaded, the feet
that fled. I repeat —

These are the pumps
with heels like young stumps,
the arches so harrow,
the toes rather narrow.
O Gentles! O Frumps!
Yes, these are the pumps
and these are the pumps
and these are the pumps that Jane wore.

Old Woman

There was an old woman
named Nothing-To-You
who dwelled in a hillside
and tended her stew
and minded her children:
they were not a few;
and minded her business.
It's nothing to you.

There was an old woman
named Nothing-To-Me
who wore an old bonnet,
one rose and a bee,
a new-mended apron
at quarter to three,
and a gardening glove
when she poured the bohea.

There was an old woman
named Nothing-To-Do
who drove to Miami
and rented a shoe
by the greebious ocean,
two rheums and a view —
and wintered on peanuts
and pigeon ragout.

There was an old woman
named Nothing-To-See
who dug a neat hole,
called it Fiddle-de-dee.
She bowed to the neighbors.
She bowed to the sea.
Then she watered the cat,
but that's nothing to me.

O it's nothing to you
and it's nothing to me
that there's nothing to do
and there's nothing to see;
that nothing is new
and we've nothing but trouble.
We bob on the stew.
All the world is a bubble.
Old woman says, "Nibble.
A crust for Aunt Sybil?"

Limerick Hagiograph

I rejoiced when I heard the good news
had converted the Romans and Jews.
    O immackeral song!
    Alas — something went wrong,
and St Louis gave birth to the blues.

I. "Let's praise sweet umbellicle Pi,"
sang St Timothy Welkin of Skye
    hymning roundly (*Hosanna!*)
    God's piping, hot manna
at crossroads and corners, "Who'll buy?"

As St Butterbaugh sat by a river
an indecorous bliss like a quiver
    possessed him. He sang,
    "It's a spiritual gang
that flows from my bowels and liver."

St Troubador sang Holy Mary
and performed a remote sort of raree
    on a very high wire
    with thighs like a lyre
and a lyrical voice like raspberry.

Remember St Flagella stripping
to apples and honey bees, whipping
    her knees in the orchard.
    What prettily tortured
expressions! like Agatha nipping.

As they flew in the nude through St Pete's,
acrobatical, plucked paracletes —
    "Divine love sometimes feels
    oddly head over heels,"
said St Spats. Said St Sparrow, "Toot, Sweets!"

II. What a hullaballoo at the Deli!
Rash sainthood's afflicted our Nellie.
    Such gothic excesses!
    Monastic MS's,
stigmatic, transfigure her belly.

St Bridgit, recovering dipso,
was saved by a sunburnt Calypso,
    converted from voodoo,
    who preached in the nude — OO!
a spirited *de facto ipso*.

Lord Bugbear reported: "Androgenous
Pips in the Washout. Erogenous
    Zoons — stand alerted —
    confirmed and converted
by God's pilgrim, St Humperdink Progenous."

St Stigmat will never be wed.
He has lost his betrothed. As she said,
    "I'll not marry a lout
    with his bones sticking out
and ninety-nine holes in his head."

"Heigh-ho!" said St Ethica frying
at stake and ascended espying
    her lord. To her foes
    she cried, "Hoopla!" and rose,
triumphant, with buttresses flying.

III. Ah pretty! St Ubisunt Noodle,
impertinent mystic *von Doodle*
   am Dawdle, sly needle,
   embroidered a beadle
and crewelled the Pope's pinky poodle.

"Our Abbess, got riotous fat,
tumbles regular down — pit-a-pat —
   to the vats. What a racket
   of beads — scatty placket!"
said St Pert as she put out the cat.

The rap — O! could not have been eerier
that knocked up our Mother Superior.
   Great Babes! In a bundle
   St Troll and St Trundle
matched heaven with lightnings interior.

As he slipped through his navel St Trots
encountered twelve pert polyglots
   and a Babel of altars
   while hermaphrodite psalters
in pews tuned subversicle plots.

St Wynnepeg Powell said, "Scat!"
to the devil. He tipped his top hat.
   As he bowed from the waist
   an ambiguous paste
greenly oozed from one glove and a spat.

IV. With a swift, predatorial claw
St Horowitz laid down the law:
    It was oval, and speckled,
    and a wee voice that heckled
inside it said, "No-no!" and "Faugh!"

Maintained at *Der Schloss von der Splenum*
St Apocrypha's odd duodenum
    is a relic that puzzles.
    It gurgles and guzzles
and spritzes a passionate venom.

"Last things!" shouted grizzled St Grump
as he straddled a quenchable lump.
    St Stumpeter, turning
    away from a burning
that quickened his peg, shouted — "Trump!"

St Rigor said, "Come — we will stomp
out the glitter and frivilous pomp
    that bedevils these sinners."
    "God give them good dinners
and generous hearts," said St Romp.

On a donkey, St Rudy Mahoney
rode out — in his fist a boloney,
    in the other a bun —
    singing "Bless everyone!"
while the donkey sang, "Hey! nonny-nony — "

The Christ

Catechism

"God's will makes good available to sense
and only in God's image can a man
have virtue. Virtue is obedience
to all God's will makes manifest." *What then?*
"God's reason, like God's will, is absolute
and willingly expressed." *Does man have reason
only in God's image?* "Yes. The fruit
may glitter, but the sun creates the season
for its ripening. God is, exists,
and only in God's image man draws breath.
Obedience is life." *If man resists,
is there no consequence?* "Vice, Madness, Death.
God's Love, Peter! What will you ask me next?"
Perhaps — you'll — explicate a sacred — text —

Religious Observation

These sixteen packs of pennies
wrapped in purple look
like statuary shrouded
during Lent.

Carol

While children, plump and white and nimble,
hand in hand parade their simple
circles on the green and gambol,
sunlight sings in every dimple.

The fiddler, brown in leather pants,
excites the children to their dance.
The buttons on his coat, immense,
are green as forests, gay as France.
   While children, plump and white and nimble,
   arm in arm parade their simple
   circles on the green and gambol,
   sunlight sings in every dimple.

Bow-legged fiddler merrily warms
the children to their leaping swarms,
   informs their wreathing.
How busily he bows his arms
and bows his waist as he performs
   upon their breathing.
   While children, plump and white and nimble,
   arm in arm parade their simple
   circles on the green and gambol,
   sunlight sings in every dimple.

Pearl-eyed, the fiddler, bending alone,
turns on the children the yellow-white stone
   from his eyelid glowing.
No paler glow the sky has shown.
It seems as if, upon the moon,
   white snow were snowing while the children,
   plump and white and nimble,
   hand in hand parade their simple
   circles on the green. They scramble
   and sunlight swallows every dimple.

Two Legends: (1) A Birthday Party

When the baby was wrapped and laid,
brown pigeons gathered. They nested in the rafters.
Blue pigeons gathered nesting in the rafters.
White pigeons gathered nesting overhead.
Pigeons slept and watched.

Saint Simple can see many brown pigeons.
Saint Simple sees blue pigeons.
He sees white pigeons overhead.
All saints have pigeons in their eyes.
Saint Simple has brown pigeons.

Cows stand behind them lowing.
They are rectangular with great round eyes.
Cows straddle dung and stare.
Saint Simple sees two cows.
The donkey also has round eyes.
His eyes look very softly.
The donkey does not stare.
The donkey does not stare but cares.
He cares as he carried.
He carried them the way.
As they came his eyes grew softer.
He became softer and softer.
Finally he was very careful.

Straw lay gleaming all around them.
Straw makes high bright corners.
It draws light and seems to breathe.
All saints share warm straw.
The donkey has his share.
Saint Simple sees them watching and staring,
discovering his lively cross beneath the straw,
believing this straw must be roses.

The donkey's ears are tall.
Tall ears do have a gentle shape.
The pigeons seem to listen.
They see the sky with one eye.
The other turns downward listening.
The cows undoubtedly can hear the singing.

There is singing afar and lively silence.
Eyes and ears attend events in stables.
The baby cries or snores.
His snores keep wonderful rhythm.
They join the singing that comes closer.
His cry is also lively.
The silence is very lively.
Straw breathes still more carefully.

Many newly have been coming.
All the while there has been singing.
Shepherds look in with shepherdesses.
They have lively brown faces.
Lily comes with lovely shepherds.

All saints are naturally pleased with shepherds.
Lambs leap among their legs.
Lambs warm their brown necks.
Brown lambs and sack cover broad shoulders.
Lively arms cradle their lambs.
Shepherds and their lambs keep warm together.
Shepherds are certainly a pleasure for saints.

Angels sing overhead from afar.
Mary is happy to smile at shepherds.
Angels sing from the rafters.
Pigeons fly out and return.
Shepherds are shyly happy listening to angels.
Mary listens naturally to angels.
Blue pigeons whisper to her.
Pigeons gather naturally at her elaborate belly.

They flock about her carefully.
She cares as she carried.
She carried while they came from afar.
Her belly carried the cross.
Her belly grew with it merrily rising.
Saint Simple listens naturally.
Lily naturally listens.
Lily and Saint Simple listen naturally to angels.
Everyone takes pleasure that her belly grew.

Her belly rose merrily arisen.
Angels sing a wholly new prayer.
Among all stars grows a new star.
Angels bring it here singing.
Angels have carried a star.

Westward camels carried eastern kings from afar.
They brought gifts very merrily.
Having a certain intelligence they look carefully.
They stand lively inside themselves.
Shepherds look on with lively brown faces.
Here is gold and crosses.
Here is frankincense and crosses.
Here is gold, myrrh, frankincense and crosses.
Saint Simple cares for spices.
He carries his lively cross.

Many ears attend the cries that sing.
His snores are like prayers.
Golden straw covers everyone gladly.
All saints take pleasure coming into stables.
Everyone naturally likes it warm.

Dawn makes a different kind of morning.
Roosters crow a different morning.
Angels sing and roosters crow.
Here is crowing and crowding.
Saint Simple sees the morning is announced.
The baby is attended at his lively coming.

Two Legends: (2) Nails

In the morning while elaborate cumuli swelled higher
Saint Simple clenching four great nails in his teeth
hammered the right hand to the cross.
He held the second nail O! so precisely in place
on the palm of the left hand feeling the flesh
and the warm blood spurting.
The warm blood brightening
in sunlight splattered his lively face
as he hammered the left foot to the cross.
As he hammered the right foot to the cross Saint Simple
saw the great nail glittering in sunlight turn
black slowly into roses' thorns.

A great many pigeons came soaring above swelling
cumuli, glittering beneath cumuli, round cumuli darting
in and out of elaborate cumuli. Many
blue pigeons soaring above swelling cumuli
came glittering beneath the cumuli,
came, white pigeons soaring above the cumuli filling
the whole sky, darting in and flashing out of cumuli.
A great many pigeons suddenly were pinned to the sky.

When Lily, the great nail glittering, hammered
the right hand to the cross she saw the fingers
close upon it as if accepting a gift.
When Lily hammered the left hand to the cross
she saw the fingers close around it tenderly
as if they wished to keep it always.
Lily had laid the nails in a neat row
in the sunshine with the grass
blowing around them, the third nail for the left foot.
She pounded the nail into the right foot, pounded
the nail, pounded the nail, pounded
the nail and hammered the right foot to the cross.

Beneath bright cumuli
where pigeons were pinned to the sky
Lily held the nail on the palm of the hand, Saint Simple
hammering then the right and then
the left hand to the cross, Lily
excellently holding the nails in place
in the sunshine. Saint Simple and Lily
were together and serious
singers hammering the left foot then.
Although Lily polished them very industriously to a finish,
when Saint Simple drove the nail into the right foot then,
the nails blackened to roses' thorns.

All night Bright Tiger
labored with the slender body and the cross,
driving the nails straight through simple flesh,
both hands and feet. The right hand first
he hammered to the cross and the left then,
his only light the blood. The blood dripping
like a glowing jewel, Tiger hammered. A great
nail began glowing, the left foot glowing.
He hammered the right foot to the cross and saw
the cross glow crimson against black grass like flame
or a superb rose. And as the flaming of the wounds
grew higher brightness spread across the forest
to the black thief hanging.

The black thief hanging is not singing,
but he is murmuring very much like singing,
and Tiger begins his digging. In the long night,
silent with the thief's singing, Tiger digs
the middle of the clearing. Tiger drags
the cross with its flaming burden. Tiger lifts
the whole cross making a glowing trail across the sky.

The red blood, very much like singing,
very much like burdens, seems flaming
or a superb rose. It is a rose,
superb rose glowing against black sky and vast trees.
Its thorns are very black and in the middle
of the clearing in the middle
of the forest it is
a rose, a rose.

In the sunlight little boys, twelve
little boys in the careful sunlight, gathered
and hammered the right hand to the cross,
yellow hair hanging down. They hammered
the tender left hand to the cross and the yellow
hair hanging was like bees humming. Twelve
little girls in white then hammered the lively
left foot to the cross with their white frocks
gleaming in the careful sunlight. Their hair whipping
widely around their golden faces, they hammered
the right foot to the cross and the yellow
hair whipping was like rain blowing.

Their yellow hair humming like bees,
hair blowing like rain,
they gathered there and then
they pinned bright pigeons to the sky.
The nails became roses' thorns.
The wounds became roses.
The children reflect,
reflect, reflect
roses and roses
and roses.

Seven Salvations:
A Mixed Bag

Sweet Jesus made the skies
to worship me. Bright eyes
flash round me like Pathé
all night. And every day
I'm news skimming the spot-
lit top off the world's love pot,
creampuff & horse & booze
& rave reviews & blues.
Sweet — oh he lets me run
my ass off! takes me down
softly, softly, & lays
his earthy foot like praise
on my scared stomach. "Lo —"
he whispers. His big toe
just nicely curls into
my navel. "Look — it's you —"

Sweet Jesus knows I'm right.
He joins me & we fight
together for fair shakes,
straight odds, & even breaks;
assures me on the field:
"I also love the world."
When evening comes he'll toss
the planets & stars across
the sky like marbles, nod
proudly while I play god
between his knees. I drift
off slowly. Then he'll lift
me up & tuck me in
with thunder round my chin.

Sweet Jesus is a man.
He shouts across the span
of ages, "Woman!" Comes
naked, swinging his plums,
to meet me. Here we stand.
He drops his own swift hand.
The Adam tree uproots
to hang me with those fruits.
Bleeding he stands & waits
for me to part the gates
of pearl & then we pass
abreast on moonlit grass.

Sweet Jesus at the bank
welcomes my corporate rank.
He is the perfect teller.
Modest as Rockefeller
he slides a golden wheat
across the bar. "Take. Eat."
It's good to know that grace
earns interest & place
is kept in Paradise.
We're sure it's very nice.

Sweet Jesus does not sneer
or shun me because I'm queer.
He feeds my boyish need
his manhood. Like a steed
he rides me. Like a sheep
he bears me. While I sleep,
surfeited, he brings
me out on fairy wings
as public as a gem
in heaven's diadem.

Sweet Jesus' tears are wine.
He is the living vine.
He finds me in the john.
I rest my mouth upon
his wounds. He has no shame.
He knows the devil's name
and calls him out. Next thing —
while jukebox angels sing
we're dancing on a sea
of grapes like Galilee.
The waves splash up & stain
our faces like spring rain
& I'm plowed. Like a boy
the turned earth guzzles joy.

Sweet Jesus puts the lights
out, stills the hectic flights
of angels in my breast,
stifles, & lets me rest.
Together by our heels
we hang. The cosmos reels
& dies. While heaven hollows,
heaves, & the green world follows
fading spark after spark,
Sweet Jesus keeps the dark.